CW01065001

Short Giraffe means high quality children's books.

Jokes Books Coloring Books Riddles for Kids Books Activity Books Quiz Books

...and everything that's meant for children!

Like us so you don't miss any news!

https://fb.me/shortgiraffebooks

Contact us
https://m.me/shortgiraffebooks

If you like this book, please consider leaving a review.

This Book Belongs To

_____

_____

Table Of Content

(Also called "TOC")

KNOCK-KNOCK JOKES

Knock-knock.

Who's there?

Annie.

Annie who?

Annie thing you do is fine for me, just open the door.

Knock-knock.

Who's there?

Lena.

Lena who?

Len-a little closer, and I'll tell you more jokes!

Knock-knock.

Who's there?

Wa.

Wa who?!

What are you so excited about?!

Knock-knock.

Who's there?

Adore.

Adore who?

A-dore is between me and you, so please open it!

Knock-knock.

Who's there?

I am.

I am who?

Don't you even know who you are?!

Knock-knock.

Who's there?

A leaf.

A leaf... who?

A leaf you alone only if you leaf me alone.

Knock-knock.

Who's there?

Candice.

Candice who?

Can-dice joke get any worse?!

Knock-knock.

Who's there?

Ice cream soda.

Ice cream soda who?

I-ce cream so-da people can hear me!

Knock-knock.

Who's there?

Olive.

Olive who?

O-live next door. Hi neighbor!

Knock-knock.

Who's there?

Nun.

Nun who?

Nun of your business!

Knock-knock.

Who's there?

Hawaii.

Hawaii who?

I'm fine, Haw-aii you?

Knock-knock.

Who's there?

June.

June who?

June-know how long I've been here knocking your door? 😠 🙁

Knock-knock.

Who's there?

Dwayne.

Dwayne who?

Dwayne the bathtub, I'm DWOwning!

Knock-knock.

Who's there?

Bed.

Bed who?

Bed you can't guess who I am!

Knock-knock.

Who's there?

Billy James Antoniazzi.

Billy James Antoniazzi who?

Are you serious? How many Billy James Antoniazzi do you know?

Knock-knock.

Who's there?

Theodore.

Theodore who?

Theo-dore wasn't opened... So, I knocked.

Knock-knock.

Who's there?

Alec.

Alec who?

A-lec it when you ask me questions. ☺

Knock-knock.

Who's there?

Canoe.

Canoe who?

Can-oe come and play with me? I'm bored!

Knock-knock.

Who's there?

Europe.

Europe who?

No, I'm not a poo. YOU're a poo!

Knock-knock.

Who's there?

Double.

Double who?

W!

Knock-knock.

Who's there?

I am.

I am who?

Again? Mmh... I think you have identity problems, huh?

Knock-knock.

Who's there?

Interrupting sloth.

Interrupting sloth who?

... (20 seconds of silence) ...

Slooooooooooth!

Knock-knock.

Who's there?

Ida.

Ida who?

Sure! It's a U.S. state and it's pronounced "Idaho".

Knock-knock.

Who's there?

Cabbage.

Cabbage who?

Do you really expect a cabbage to have a last name?

Knock-knock.

Who's there?

Sweden.

Sweden who?

Sweden sour chicken!

Knock-knock.

Who's there?

Art.

Art who?

R2-D2, of course! 🤖

Knock-knock.

Who's there?

Smellmop.

Smellmop who?

Ew, no thanks... I'd rather not smell it. ☝️

Knock-knock.

Who's there?

Tank.

Tank who?

You're welcome!

Knock-knock.

Who's there?

Voodoo.

Voodoo who?

Voo-doo you think you are?? Don't ask me so many questions.

Knock-knock.

Who's there?

Opportunity.

...

... Opportunity doesn't knock twice!

Knock-knock.

Who's there?

Butter.

Butter who?

We'd butter be quick, we don't have much time!

FUNNY KNOCK-KNOCK JOKES

Knock-knock.

Who's there?

Says.

Says who?

Says me, that's who!

Knock-knock.

Who's there?

Dishes.

Dishes who?

Dishes the police, open up!

Knock-knock.

Who's there?

Lettuce.

Lettuce who?

As I said: Lett-uce in immediately, or we will break down the door!

Knock-knock.

Who's there?

Luke.

Luke who?

Luke through the keyhole and you see!

Knock-knock.

Who's there?

Odysseus.

Odysseus who?

O... dyss-eus the last straw!! 😠

Knock-knock.

Who's there?

A Mayan.

A Mayan who?

A Mayan in the way?

Knock-knock.

Who's there?

Abe.

Abe who?

Abe-C-D-E!

Knock-knock.

Who's there?

Gorilla.

Gorilla who?

Gorilla me a hamburger, please!

Knock-knock.

Who's there?

Snow.

Snow who?

Snow use, I forgot my name again. 😑

Knock-knock.

Who's there?

Ya.

Ya who?

No thanks, I prefer to use Bing or Google.

Knock-knock.

Who's there?

Robin. 🏹

Robin who?

Robin you! Now hand over the cash! 🔫

Knock-knock.

Who's there?

Tennis. 🎾

Tennis who?

Tenn-is five plus five! `10` = `5` + `5`

Knock-knock.

Who's there?

Figs.

Figs who?

Figs the doorbell, it's not working!

Knock-knock.

Who's there?

Cow says.

Cow says who?

No, a cow says *MOOOOO!*

Knock-knock.

Who's there?

Hal.

Hal who?

Hal can you know if you don't open this door first?

Knock-knock.

Who's there?

Woo.

Woo who?!

Glad you're excited, too!

Knock-knock.

Who's there?

Claire.

Claire who?

Claire the way, I'm coming in!

Knock-knock.

Who's there?

Gladys.

Gladys, who?

Gladys the weekend—no homework! 🔲 🔲 👻 ✖

Knock-knock.

Who's there?

Ho Ho.

Ho Ho who?

Hey dude, your Santa Claus impression needs some work. 🔔

Knock-knock.

Who's there?

Abel.

Abel who?

Abel to see you through this peephole!

Knock-knock.

Who's there?

A short girl.

A short girl who?

A short girl who can't reach the doorbell!

Knock-knock.

Who's there?

Cheese.

Cheese who?

For cheese a jolly good fellow.

Knock-knock.

Who's there?

Hans.

Hans who?

Hans off my Easter candy!

Knock-knock.

Who's there?

Frank!

Frank who?

Frank you very much for being my friend!

Knock-knock.

Who's there?

Iguana.

Iguana who?

Ig-uana hold your hand.

SUPER FUNNY KNOCK-KNOCK JOKES

Knock-knock.

Who's there?

Donut.

Donut who?

Donut ask, it's a secret!

Knock-knock.

Who's there?

Kiwi.

Kiwi who?

Ki-wi go to the store?

Knock-knock.

Who's there?

Orange.

Orange who?

Orange you sick of these knock-knock jokes yet?

Knock-knock.

Who's there?

Turnip.

Turnip who?

Turn-ip the volume, it's too quiet in here. 🔊

Knock-knock.

Who's there?

Alma.

Alma who?

Alma not going to say.

Knock-knock.

Who's there?

Amy.

Amy who?

Amy fraid, I've forgotten!

Knock-knock.

Who's there?

Barbie.

Barbie Who?

Barbie-Q Chicken!

Knock-knock.

Who's there?

Ken.

Ken who?

Ken I come in? It's freezing out here! ❄️

Knock-knock.

Who's there?

Water.

Water who?

Wat-er you doing in my house? 🏠

Knock-knock.

Who's there?

Nana.

Nana who?

Nana your business!

Knock-knock.

Who's there?

Needle.

Needle who?

Needle little help right now! Could you come out?

Knock-knock.

Who's there?

Ada.

Ada who?

Ada sandwich for lunch!

Knock-knock.

Who's there?

Sam.

Sam who?

Maybe sam day you'll recognize me!

Knock-knock.

Who's there?

Dozen.

Dozen who?

Dozen anyone want to let me in?

Knock-knock.

Who's there?

Thermos.

Thermos who?

Ther-mos be a better way to get to you...

Knock-knock.

Who's there?

Alec.

Alec who?

Alectricity.... BUZZZ! ⚡

Knock-knock.

Who's there?

Amarillo.

Amarillo who?

Am-a-rillo nice person.

Knock-knock.

Who's there?

Police.

Police who?

Police let me in, it's chilly out!

Knock-knock.

Who's there?

Ice cream.

Ice cream who?

Ice cream if you don't give me a gift!

Knock-knock.

Who's there?

Etch.

Etch who?

Bless you! 😩

Knock-knock.

Who's there?

Boo.

Boo who?

Hey, don't cry, it's just a joke!

Knock-knock.

Who's there?

Stopwatch. ⏱

Stopwatch who?

Stopwatch you're doing and let me in!

Knock-knock.

Who's there?

Icy.

Icy who?

Icy you looking at me!

Knock-knock.

Who's there?

Mary.

Mary who?

Mary Christmas!

Knock-knock.

Who's there?

I need a puh.

I need a puh-who?

Then, why don't you find a toilet!

Knock-knock.

Who's there?

Iva.

Iva who?

Iva sore hand from knocking so long!

Knock-knock.

Who's there?

Ketchup.

Ketchup who?

Ketch-up with me and I'll tell you!

Knock-knock.

Who's there?

Wooden shoe.

Wooden shoe who?

Wooden shoe like to hear another joke?

SOME CHILLOUT WITH... JOKES.

Why did the scarecrow keep getting promoted?

Because he was outstanding *in his field*!

Jokes about teachers on summer break are not funny.

They're just... *not working*!

You know how you call someone who wears a belt with a watch attached?

A *waist* of time! 🕐 🕰 ⏳

What do computers snack on?

Micro-chips! 🍟

I dig, we dig, she dig, you dig, they dig...!

This poem it's not so great, but it's definitely *very deep!* ⛏⛏

A horse walks into a bar.

The bartender says, "Why the *long face*?"

If you're feeling depressed in the middle of winter, take some butter and chuck it out the window.

...So you'll see a *butter-fly!* 🦋

Somebody stole all my lamps.

I couldn't be more *de-lighted!* 💡

Did you know about the man who broke his left arm and also his left leg?

Yes, I did 🙁 but He's all *right* now!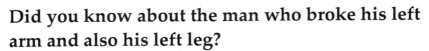

Three guys walk into a bar.

They all said: "ouch!" – it was a *hard, steel bar.*

What does the cop say to his belly button in the morning?

"You're under *a-vest!*"

Why don't teddy bears ever order dessert?

Because they're always *stuffed*!

37 consonants, 25 vowels, a question mark, and a comma went to court.

They will be *sentenced* next Friday!

How do you make a squid laugh?

With *ten-tickles*.

How can you call an alligator in a vest? 🐊

An *in-vest-igator*.

What does a pizza say when it introduces itself to you?

Slice to meet you.

Do you like wind turbines ?

Yep! I'm a big *fan*.

Why is a piano so hard to open?

Because the *keys* are on the inside.

What's the most musical bone?

The trom-*bone*.

What makes music on your hair?

A *headband*.

What's the music the balloons are afraid of?

Pop music.

What do you obtain if you cross a pie with a snake?

A *pie-thon*. 🐍

Where do cows go for entertainment?

To the *mooo-vies!*

What's the definition of *illegal?*

A sick bird.

(Eagle)

I love Switzerland.

I really don't know what is the coolest thing about that country, but their flag is a *big plus!*

Why did the M&M go to college?

Because he wanted to be a *Smarty.*

What country did candy come from?

From *Sweeten*!

What is an astronauts favourite chocolate?

A *Mars* bar.

Why did the turkey cross the road?

To prove he wasn't a *chicken*.

What do you say to a bunny when it's his birthday?

HOppy Birthday.

Why did the golfer always carry a second pair of pants?

In case he got a *hole*-in-one.

Why do fish live in saltwater?

Because pepper makes them sneeze!

What did a pizza say to a delicious topping?

I never *sau-sage* a beautiful face!

Where did the sheep go on vacation?

The *Baaaaaahamas!*

Why did the phone wear glasses?

Because it lost all its ....*contacts.*

Yesterday I was in a store that was giving away dead batteries.

They were *free of charge*.

You know, I'd like to be paid to sleep!

Wow... It would be a *dream* job.

How does a scientist freshen her breath?

With *experi-mints*.

WOW! MORE KNOCK-KNOCK JOKES!

Knock-knock.

Who's there?

Watson.

Watson who?

Watson TV right now? 📺

Knock-knock.

Who's there?

Sho Mia.

Sho Mia who?

- W H O -

Knock-knock.

Who's there?

Otto.

Otto who?

Otto know what's taking you so long!

Knock-knock.

Who's there?

Norma Lee.

Norma Lee who?

Norma-Lee I don't knock on doors, but I must see you!

Knock-knock.

Who's There?

Imma.

Imma who?

Imma growing older waiting for you out here.

Knock-knock.

Who's there?

Yukon.

Yukon who?

Yukon say that again!?

Yukon who?

Knock-knock.

Who's there?

Viper.

Viper who?

Viper nose, it's running!

Knock-knock.

Who's there?

CDs.

CDs who?

C-Ds person on your doorstep? It's me.

Knock-knock.

Who's there?

Roach.

Roach who?

Roach you a text. Did you get it?

Knock-knock.

Who's there?

Somebody too short to ring the doorbell!

Knock-knock.

Who's there?

Harry.

Harry who?

Harry up, it's cold outside!

Knock-knock.

Who's there?

Ivor.

Ivor who?

Ivor you let me in, or I'll have to climb through the window!

Knock-knock.

Who's there?

Abbot.

Abbot who?

Abbot you don't know who this is!

Knock-knock.

Who's there?

Justin.

Justin who?

Just-in time for dinner. 🍽

Knock-knock.

Who's there?

Sadie.

Sadie who?

Sadie magic word and I'll come in!

Knock-knock.

Who's there?

Iona.

Iona who?

Ion-a new toy!

Knock-knock.

Who's there?

Two knee.

Two knee who?

Two-knee fish!

Knock-knock.

Who's there?

Abby.

Abby who?

Abby birthday to you!

Knock-knock.

Who's there?

Ben.

Ben who?

Ben knocking for 10 minutes already!

Knock-knock.

Who's there?

Aida.

Aida who?

Aida sandwich for lunch today.

Knock-knock.

Who's there?

Scold.

Scold who?

S-cold enough out here to go ice skating!

Knock-knock.

Who's there?

Amanda.

Amanda who?

A-man-da fix your door!

Knock-knock.

Who's there?

Al.

Al who?

Al give you a big hug if you open the door!

Knock-knock.

Who's there?

Alien.

Alien who?

Umh.. how many aliens do you know?

Knock-knock.

Who's there?

Andrew.

Andrew who?

An-drew you a picture! Wanna see it?

Knock-knock.

Who's there?

Armageddon.

Armageddon who?

Arma-gedd(i)n a little bored. Let's go out.

Knock-knock.

Who's there?

Nobel.

Nobel who?

Nobel...that's why I knocked!

Knock-knock.

Who's there?

Goliath.

Goliath who?

Go-li*ath* down, you look*eth* tired!

Knock-knock.

Who's there?

Big interrupting cow.

Big interrupting cow who?

MOOOOOO!

(The "MOOOOOO" must be said while the other person is still asking "big interrupting cow who?")

Knock-knock.

Who's there?

Mikey.

Mikey who?

Mikey doesn't fit in the key hole!

EVEN MORE KNOCK-KNOCK JOKES!

Knock-knock.

Who's there?

Anita.

Anita who?

A-nit-a drink of water, so please let me in!

Knock-knock.

Who's there?

Banana. 🍌

Banana who?

Knock-knock.

Who's there?

Banana. 🍌

Banana who?

Knock-knock.

Who's there?

Orange. 🍊

Orange who?

Orange you glad I didn't say Banana?

Knock-knock.

Who's there?

Alex.

Alex who?

A-lex-plain when you open the door!

Knock-knock.

Who's there?

Anee.

Anee who?

Anee one you like!

Knock-knock.

Who's there?

A herd.

A herd who?

A herd you were back home, so I came to see you.

Knock-knock.

Who's there?

Avenue.

Avenue who?

Aven-ue knocked on this door before?

Knock-knock.

Who's there?

Althea.

Althea who?

Althea later alligator!

Knock-knock.

Who's there?

Doctor.

Doctor who?

Hey, you've seen that TV show?

Knock-knock.

Who's there?

Candice.

Candice who?

Can-dice door open, or am I stuck out here?

Knock-knock.

Who's there?

Justin.

Justin who?

Just-in the neighborhood and thought I'd come over!

Knock-knock.

Who's there?

Nuisance.

Nuisance who?

What's new since yesterday?

Knock-knock.

Who's there?

Cargo.

Cargo who?

No, car go BEEP BEEP!

Knock-knock.

Who's there?

Ida!

Ida who?

Ida wanna clean my room!

Knock-knock.

Who's there?

Isabel.

Isabel who?

Is-a-bel working? I had to knock! 🔔

Knock-knock.

Who's there?

Emoji.

Emoji who?

No!... Emoji Poo!

Knock-knock.

Who's there?

Alpaca.

Alpaca who?

Alpaca the suitcase, you load the car!

Knock-knock.

Who's there?

You.

You who?

How nice! I didn't think you'd be so happy to meet me!

Knock-knock.

Who's there?

Berry.

Berry who?

Berry nice too meet you. Can I come in now?

Knock-knock.

Who's there?

Broken pencil. ✏️

Broken pencil who?

Oh, never mind... it's pointless!

Knock-knock.

Who's there?

Icing.

Icing who?

I-cing very loud, so everyone can hear me!

Knock-knock.

Who's there?

Yah.

Yah who?

Wow, I'm glad you're so excited to see me again!

Knock-knock.

Who's there?

Shelby.

Shelby who?

She'll be here in a few moments.

Knock-knock.

Who's there?

Anita.

Anita who?

Ooopen pleeease! A-ni-ta go to the bathroom!

Knock-knock.

Who's there?

Time.

Time who?

Time for dinner, it's getting late. Are you inviting me to eat?

Knock-knock.

Who's there?

Tennis.

Tennis who?

Tennis-see!

Knock-knock.

Who's there?

Hubie.

Hubie who?

Hubie-ginning to understand how these jokes work?

Knock-knock.

Who's there?

Holly.

Holly who?

Holly-days **are here again!**

Knock-knock.

Who's there?

Irish stew.

Irish stew, who?

I-rish stew in the name of the law.

Knock-knock.

Who's there?

Judo.

Judo who?

What, Ju-do know?

CRAZY KNOCK-KNOCK JOKES

Knock-knock.

Who's there?

Alice.

Alice who?

Alice so quiet. Let's make some noise!

Knock-knock.

Who's there?

Euripides.

Euripides who?

Eu-ripides my jeans and now you pay for them, okay???

Knock-knock.

Who's there?

Amash.

Amash who?

Really, you're a shoe? Uh... okay.

Knock-knock.

Who's there?

Sing.

Sing who?

Whooooooo! 🎵🎵

Knock-knock.

Who's there?

Irish.

Irish who?

Irish you would stop talking.

Knock-knock.

Who's there?

Bach.

Bach who?

Bach, bach... I'm a chicken.

Knock-knock.

Who's there?

Elmo.

Elmo who?

You don't know who Elmo is?!

Knock-knock.

Who's there?

FBI.

FBI w-

We're asking the questions here.

Knock-knock.

Who's there?

Major.

Major who?

Major day with this joke haven't I?

Knock-knock.

Who's there?

Control Freak.

Co—

Ok, you should say "Control freak who" now.

Knock-knock.

Who's there?

Owls say.

Owls say who? 🦉

Yes, they do. But I still need to come in.

Knock-knock.

Who's there?

Want.

Want who?

Want, who, want who three four!

Knock-knock.

Who's there?

Kenya.

Kenya who?

Ken-ya let me in already?

Knock-knock.

Who's there?

Sacha.

Sacha who?

Sacha lot of questions!

Knock-knock.

Who's there?

Les.

Les who?

Les go out!

Knock-knock.

Who's there?

Egg.

Egg who?

I'm Egg-stremely disappointed you don't recognize me 😞

Knock-knock.

Who's there?

Sherwood.

Sherwood who?

Sherwood like you to open the door!

Knock-knock.

Who's there?

Kanga.

Kanga who?

It's pronounced kangaroo, actually. 🐱

Knock-knock.

Who's there?

Iran.

Iran who?

I-ran really fast to come here to see you.

Knock-knock.

Who's there?

Max.

Max who?

Max no difference, open the door!

Knock-knock.

Who's there?

Noah.

Noah who?

Noah way I can get in?

Knock-knock.

Who's there?

Jess.

Jess who?

Jess open the door!

Knock-knock.

Who's there?

Sarah.

Sarah who?

Sa-rah phone I could use here?

Knock-knock.

Who's there?

Déjà.

Déjà who?

Knock-knock.

Knock-knock.

Who's there?

Radio.

Radio who?

Radi-o not, I'm going in anyway!

Knock-knock.

Who's there?

Passion.

Passion who?

Pass-ion by, and thought I'd pop in!

Knock-knock.

Who's there?

Milky.

Milky who?

Milky way!

Knock-knock.

Who's there?

Suspense.

Suspense who?

...

...

...

... It's just me.

A LITTLE BREAK
WITH DUMB JOKES

What do you call a thieving alligator?

A *crook-o-dile*.

What time should we go to the dentist?

At *tooth hurt-y*

(2:30)

How do you stop an elephant from charging?

By taking his *credit cards* away.

What time does a duck wake up?

At the *quack* of dawn!

What dog keeps the best time?

A *watch* dog!

What has fangs and webbed feet?

Count *Duckula*.

You know why cats are so good at videogames?

Because they have *nine lives*.

Why can't a leopard hide?

Because he's always *spotted*.

What do dogs do when they want to stop watching a Netflix movie?

They press the *"paws"* button.

Why the banana had to go to the hospital?

It was not *peeling* very well.

What vitamin helps you to see?

Vitamin "C". 👁 👁

Why was the musician arrested?

Because she got in *treble*.

Why did the icecream cone take judo lessons?

It was tired of getting *licked*.

Why did the belt go to jail?

He held up a pair of pants. 🩳

How do barbers speed up their job?

They take *short-cuts*.

Why don't skeletons go to dance?

They have *no-body* to go with.

What stays in the corner but goes around the world?

A stamp. ✉

What goes up but never comes down?

Your age.

Why was the math book so sad?

It had too many *problems.*

Why did the hen go to school?

To take her *Eggsam*. ◯

What's the first thing just married rabbits do?

They go on a *bunny-moon*. 🐰 🖤 🐰

Why did the student eat his homework?

Because the teacher at school said it was a *piece of cake*.

Where do mummies go swimming?

The *Dead Sea*.

What kind of table can you eat?

A *vege-table*.

How does a lion greet other animals in wild?

Nice to *eat* you.

What kind of tree can you put in your hand?

A palm tree.

What do you call a boomerang that doesn't work?

A stick. 😖

What kind of candy

is never on time?

Choco-late.

Why did the melon jump in the lake.

He wanted to be a *water-melon*.

Do you know why the football coach walks into the bank?

To get his *quarter-back*.

What is that animal that can jump higher than a house?

Any animal. A house can't jump. 😬

How do you spot a modern spider?

He doesn't have a web, he has his own *website*. 🕷

What are the strongest creatures in the ocean?

Mussels

When do astronauts eat?

At *launch* time. 🚀

What part of your car is always tired?

The *exhaust* pipe!

Do you know what they call a dinosaur that takes a nap?

A *dino-snore*.

What do you call a well-dressed ant?

Eleg-ant. 🦃 💂 ♣

My dog can do magic tricks.

It's a *labracadabrador*.

I tried to grab the fog.

I *mist*.

I opened my wardrobe, and I found a big lion inside! So, I asked why he was there !?

...he said it was "*Narnia* Business".

I just came back from a once-in-a-lifetime vacation...

Nice ! Did you enjoy it?

I tell you what: *never again.*

CRAZY JOKES ABOUT... SOMEONE KNOCKING ON THE DOOR!

Knock-knock.

Who's there?

Tyrone.

Tyrone who?

Tyrone shoelaces!

Knock-knock.

Who's there?

Wendy.

Wendy who?

Wendy bell works again, I won't have to knock.

Knock-knock.

Who's there?

Chick.

Chick who?

Chick your stove, I can smell it burning!

Knock-knock.

Who's there?

Goat. 🐐

Goat who?

Goat to the door and find out.

Knock-knock.

Who's there?

Kent.

Kent who?

Kent you tell who I am by my voice?

Knock-knock.

Who's there?

Arfur.

Arfur who?

Arfur got!

Knock-knock.

Who's there?

Oslo.

Oslo who?

O-slo down, what's the hurry!?

Knock-knock.

Who's there?

Pasture.

Pasture who?

Past-ure bedtime, isn't it?

Sdeng-Sdeng.

Who's there?

Burglar.

Burglar who?

Burglars don't knock!

Knock-knock.

Who's there?

Rough.

Rough who?

Rough, rough, rough! It's your dog!

Knock-knock.

Who's there?

Comb.

Comb who?

Comb on down, and I'll tell you!

Knock-knock.

Who's there?

Dewey.

Dewey who?

De-wey have to do this every time?

Knock-knock.

Who's there?

Leena.

Leena who?

Leen-a little closer and I'll tell you.

Knock-knock.

Who's there?

Adore.

Adore who?

A-door's still closed... open up!

Knock-knock.

Who's there?

Ray.

Ray who?

Ray-member me?

Knock-knock.

Who's there?

Me.

Me who?

Don't you know who you are?

Knock-knock.

Who's there?

Howl.

Howl who?

Howl you know if this door is still closed?

Knock-knock.

Who's there?

Haven.

Haven who?

Haven you heard enough knock-knock jokes?

Knock-knock.

Who's there?

Russell.

Russell who?

Russell up some food, I'm hungry!

Knock-knock.

Who's there?

Riot.

Riot who?

Riot on time, here I am!

Knock-knock.

Who's there?

Amish.

Amish who?

Aw, honey... A-mish you too! 🖤

Knock-knock.

Who's there?

Mango. 🥭

Mango who?

Man, go to the door and simply open it!

Knock-knock.

Who's there?

Will.

Will who?

Will you let me in already?

Knock-knock.

Who's there?

Mode.

Mode who?

Mode the lawn, because the grass is very high!

Knock-knock.

Who's there?

Panther.

Panther who?

Panth-er no panth, I'm going swimming !

BONUS! OTHER KNOCK-KNOCK JOKES!

Knock-knock.

Who's there?

Spell.

Spell who?

Ok: "W-H-O"!

Knock-knock.

Who's there?

Conrad.

Conrad who?

Conrad-ulations! That was a good knock-knock joke!

Knock-knock.

Who's there?

Amos.

Amos who?

A mosquito just bit me! ❀

Knock-knock.

Who's there?

Howard.

Howard who?

Howard I know?

Knock-knock.

Who's there?

Dejav.

Dejav who?

Knock-knock.

Knock-knock.

Who's there?

Razor.

Razor who?

Raz-or hands, it's the police!

Knock-knock.

Who's there?

Juno.

Juno who?

Juno how long I've been out here?

Knock-knock.

Who's there?

Annie.

Annie who?

Annie body home?

Knock-knock.

Who's there?

Sherlock.

Sherlock who?

Sherlock your door tight, don't you?

Knock-knock.

Who's there?

Hoo.

Hoo who?

Sorry, I thought this was my friend's house, didn't know an owl lived here. 🦉

Knock-knock.

Who's there?

Alfred.

Alfred who?

Al-fred of the dark!!

Knock-knock.

Who's there?

Honeybee.

Honeybee who?

Honeybee a dear and open the door!

Knock-knock.

Who's there?

Dozen.

Dozen who?

Dozen all this knocking bother you?

Knock-knock.

Who's there?

Venice.

Venice who?

Venice your mother coming home? I need to ask her something.

Knock-knock.

Who's there?

Mustache.

Mustache who?

I thought I must-ache you a question...

...But no problem, I can 😄shave😄 it for tomorrow!

Knock-knock.

Who's there?

Emma.

Emma who?

Emm-a bit cold, can you let me in?

Knock-knock.

Who's there?

Who

Who who?

I didn't know you were an owl!

Knock-knock.

Who's there?

Doris.

Doris who?

Dor-is locked, that's why I'm knocking!

Knock-knock.

Who's there?

Wire.

Wire who?

Wire you asking me?

Knock-knock.

Who's there?

Eye nose.

Eye nose who?

Eye nose plenty more knock-knock jokes!

Knock-knock.

Who's there?

Cash.

Cash who?

No thanks, I'm allergic to nuts.

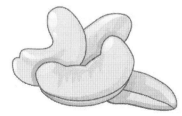

Knock-knock.

Who's there?

Canoe.

Canoe who?

Can-oe help me with my homework?

Knock-knock.

Who's there?

Henrietta.

Henrietta who?

Henri-ett-a worm that was in his apple.

Knock-knock.

Who's there?

King Tut.

King Tut who?

King Tut-key fried chicken!

Knock-knock.

Who's there?

Noah.

Noah who?

No-ah good place we can get something to eat?

Knock-knock.

Who's there?

Barry.

Barry who?

Barry the treasure where no one will find it!

Knock-knock.

Who's there?

Uganda.

Uganda who?

U-ganda get away with this!

Knock-knock.

Who's there?

Wine!

Wine who?

Wine don't you like these jokes?

THIS IS THE VERY LAST TRANCHE OF KNOCK-KNOCK JOKES!

Knock-knock.

Who's there?

From.

From who?

Grammatically speaking, you should say "from whom."

Knock-knock.

Who's there?

Witches.

Witches who?

Witch-es the way to the store?

Knock-knock.

Who's there?

Phillip!

Phillip who?

Phill-ip my bag with Halloween candy, please!

Knock-knock.

Who's there?

Ghost.

Ghost who?

Gho-stand over there, and I'll bring you some candy! 👻

Knock-knock.

Who's there?

Arthur.

Arthur who?

Ar-thur any Thanksgiving leftovers so I can eat them?

Knock-knock.

Who's there?

Esther.

Esther who?

Es-ther any more sweet potato pie?

Knock-knock.

Who's there?

Tamara.

Tamara who?

Tamara we'll have a trip to the lake.

Knock-knock.

Who's there?

Wanda.

Wanda who?

Wan-da go see a movie at the cinema?

Knock-knock.

Who's there?

Ava.

Ava who?

Ava ever seen a play about Shakespeare?

Knock-knock.

Who's there?

Ima.

Ima who?

Ima guy who's ringing your doorbell.

Knock-knock.

Who's there?

Cole.

Cole who?

Cole is not exactly what I was expecting for Christmas this year! 😲 👎

Knock-knock.

Who's there?

Yule.

Yule who?

Yule know as soon as you look out the door.

Knock-knock.

Who's there?

No one.

No one who?

** Remains silent **

Knock-knock.

Who's there?

Alaska.

Alaska who?

Al-ask-a gift from Santa Claus 🎅

Knock-knock.

Who's there?

Honedew.

Honedew who?

Ho-ned-ew to open this door for me, please.

Knock-knock.

Who's there?

Cook.

Cook who?

Hey, you really want to cook someone? You do sound crazy!

Knock-knock.

Who's there?

Noise.

Noise who?

Noise to see you!

Knock-knock.

Who's there?

Urine.

Urine who?

Ur-ine trouble if you don't open this door right now!!

Knock-knock.

Who's there?

Knock.

Knock who?

Knock-knock.

Knock-knock.

Who's there?

Disguise.

Disguise who?

Dis-guse is your boyfriend. 😊 I love you!

Knock-knock.

Who's there?

Aaaahh.

Aaaahh who?

A big wolf, I guess...

If I had to go away for a long time, would you still remember me after one year?

Yes.

And after 2 years?

Yes.

And after 5 years?

Yes.

And... what about after 10 years?

Yes, of course!

Knock-knock.

Who's there?

Well... that hurts.

Knock-knock.

Why the heck are you knocking? You're right next to me!

Knock-knock.

Who's there?

Lion.

Lion who?

Lion at your feet. Now have some heart and kiss me.

Knock-knock.

Who's there?

Maia.

Maia who?

Mai-abilities are wasted on these stupid jokes.

Knock-knock.

Who's there?

Cereal.

Cereal who?

Cereal killer. Have you been naughty or good?

Knock-knock.

Who's there?

Wire.

Wire who?

Wire we here? Why is anybody here? Let's just have a drink together.

Knock-knock.

Who's there?

Norway.

Norway who?

Nor-way to get through this door, apparently..

Knock-knock.

Who's there?

It's Britney Spears.

Britney Spears who?

Knock-knock. ♫ Oops!, I did it again. ♫

Knock-knock.

Who's there?

Gino.

Gino who?

Gin-o me, now open the door!

Knock-knock.

Who'sre?

Pasta.

Pasta who?

Past-a salt please!

Knock-knock.

Who's there?

Weevil.

Weevil who?

Tum-Tum-Cha! Tum-Tum-Cha!

Weevil Weevil Rock You !!

Knock-knock.

Who's there.

Zombies.

Zombies who?

Zom-bies make honey, and zom-bies don't.

Well, we figured out that Knock-Knock jokes are really funny! The person who invented them should definitely receive a... *No-Bell* prize.

BONUS 2! PREMIUM JOKES!!

Why did the boy take a ruler to bed?

To see *how long* he slept.

What's the only school where you have to drop out to graduate?

Skydiving school.

What do you call a funny mountain?

Hill-arious.

In what type of school do you learn how to greet people?

In *Hi* school.

Why can't fishermen be generous?

Because their business makes them *sellfish*.

I wondered why the tennisball was getting bigger...

...Then it hit me.

How do turtles talk to each other?

By using *shell* phones!

Why can't you trust atoms?

Because they *make up* everything!

Where do polar bears vote?

The North *Poll*.

What do you call a knight who is afraid to fight?

Sir Render.

Why can't a motorbike stand up by its self?

Because it's *two-tyred*

How do you cut the ocean in half?

With a *Sea-Saw*!

What did the blanket say when it fell off the bed?

Oh *sheet*!

I would say a pun about mirrors...

...but that would be a *bad reflection* of me.

I don't know any kitty jokes. 😺

Really? Are you *kitten* me right *miaow*?

Why did they kick Cinderella off the basketball team?

She ran away from the *ball*

What did the tennis ball say to the other tennis ball?

See you *round*!

Why was King Arthur's army too tired to fight?

It had too many sleepless *knights*.

I asked my French friend if she likes to play video games.

She said, "*Wii*."

The machine at the coin factory just suddenly stopped working, with no explanation.

It doesn't make any *cents*!

What a volcano say to his wife before to sleep?

I *lava* you.

A doctor got angry.

He lost all his *patients*.

What does a CIA agent do when it's time for bed?

He quickly goes *under cover*.

What does the calculator say to the math student?

You can *count* on me.

This gravity joke is not new...

...but I *fall for it* every time!

What does a pen say to another pen?

You are *INKredible*.

You know that I can organize a fantastic space party?

How can you do it?

I *plan-et*.

Two wi-fi antennas got married last Saturday.

The *reception* was fantastic.

I saw an offer in a shop yesterday: "TV for $4.50 – but the volume is stuck on maximum"

And what have you done?

Well, it was an offer that... I simply couldn't *turn down*.

I spent days making a wooden car with wooden wheels.

It just *wooden* work.

Thank you, my arms...

... for always being there *by my side*.

Why is a skeleton a bad liar?

Because you can see *right through it*.

What do you achieve when you ask a lemon for help?

A *lemonaid*.

What do elves learn in school?

The *elf*-abet.

What's a Hippie's wife called?

A *Mississippi.*

Why are Apple staff absolutely forbidden to fart in Apple stores?

Because there are no *Windows.*

What is the typical diet of a sea-monster?

Fish and *ships.* 🚢

How do monsters prefer their eggs?

TerriFRIED.

I bought a dictionary, but when I opened it, the whole book was empty, all pages blank!

There are literally *-no words-* to describe how crazy I am!

Every morning I go out for a walk, and I always get run over by the same bike: it always happens in the same place, day after day... week after week... what can I do?

Hmmh... that sounds like a seriously *vicious cycle*.

Did you hear on the news about that guy who got hit over the head with a can of Coke?

Yes, he was very lucky. It was a *soft* drink.

I'm looking for some good fish jokes.

If you know any, let *minnow*.

What do you call 2 guys who love math?

Alge-bros!

The longest I've ever gone without a joke was 7 days.

...Pretty *weak*.

Two fish are swimming, when suddenly the first of them hits a concrete wall!

He turns to the other and says, "*Dam!*"

Who is that thing that jumps from one cake to another and smells like almonds?

Tarzipan.

I really wanted an invisible shirt

but I couldn't *find* one.

HOPE TO SEE YOU SOON, BABY!

Short Giraffe means high quality children's books.

🐺 Jokes Books 🐶 Coloring Books 🐱 Riddles for Kids Books 🦋 Activity Books 🐨 Quiz Books

...and everything that's meant for children! 🦋

👍 Like us so you don't miss any news!
https://fb.me/shortgiraffebooks

 Contact us
https://m.me/shortgiraffebooks

If you like this book, please consider leaving a review.

Printed in Great Britain
by Amazon